Crikey I'm...

In Love

Other titles in the *Crikey I'm...* series

Crikey I'm A Teenager

Crikey I'm Thirty

Crikey I'm Forty

Crikey I'm Fifty

Crikey I'm Retired

Crikey I'm Getting Married

Crikey I'm A Mum

Crikey I'm A Dad

Crikey I'm A Grandparent

Crikey I'm...
In Love

Contributors

Victoria Warner
Eliza Williams

Edited by

Steve Hare

Cover Illustration by

Ian Pollock

PURPLE HOUSE

Published by Purple House Limited 1998
75 Banbury Road
Oxford OX2 6PE

© Purple House Limited 1998

Cover illustration: © Ian Pollock/The Inkshed 1998

Crikey I'm... is a trademark of Purple House Limited

A catalogue record for this book is available from the British Library

ISBN 1-84118-018-1

All rights reserved. No part of this publication may be reproduced, stored in a retrieval system, or transmitted, in any form or by any means, electronic, mechanical, photocopying, recording or otherwise, without the prior permission of the publishers.

Printed in Great Britain by
Cox and Wyman

Acknowledgements

We are grateful to everyone who helped in the compilation of this book, particularly to the following:

Stephen Franks of Franks and Franks (Design)

Inform Group Worldwide (Reproduction)

Dave Kent of the Kobal Collection

Bodleian Library, Oxford

Central Library, Oxford

British Film Institute

Liz Brown

Mark McClintock

Hannah Wren

Illustrations

Photograph of entwined legs	**3**
Arthur Hughes, *The Dial*	**6**
Vilma Banky and Rudolph Valentino in *Son of the Sheik*	**9**
Faye Dunaway and Warren Beatty in *Bonnie and Clyde*	**13**
A 1993 Dateline advertisement	**19**
The statue of Eros	**24**
The Guardian's Valentine announcements	**30**
Auguste Rodin, *The Kiss*	**34**
Humphrey Bogart and Ingrid Bergman in *Casablanca*	**38**
A 1952 Britvic advertisement	**42**

Contents

Crikey I'm In Love!   **1**

Love Story   **4**

Lipstick, Powder and Paint   **16**

Legendary Lovers   **21**

Love: It's Magic   **28**

Pucker Up   **35**

The Food of Love   **43**

Hormonally Yours   **47**

Love From...?   **52**

Crikey, I'm In Love!

Love and pain are closely connected: at least that is the inevitable conclusion anyone comes to after reading through myth, legend, folklore and history.

Cupid, or his Greek counterpart Eros, caused people to fall in love by shooting them in the heart with barbed golden arrows. Love, for the ancients, was little different from the modern-day view: it was not a rational or controllable emotion. Once struck it became a matter completely outside the victims' control – they were smitten. But Cupid was a born troublemaker. More often than not, he would deliberately target only one of the potential couple, leaving that person hopelessly infatuated with a passion that would never be returned. This winged and beautiful youth brought chaos and divine madness with every arrow. Such is love.

Virtually all literature, from Homer on, is concerned in one way or another with emotion, affairs of the heart, and events outside our control. However, for most of recorded history, marriage was the result not of overwhelming mutual passion, but purely a financial transaction between the heads of two families. The young couple would be unlikely to know each other, and would be forbidden to meet at all until the contract was fulfilled.

Thus, for much of history, and all of 'society', love was a necessarily secretive passion, or one that arose more or less by accident, between a couple resigned to making the best of their life together.

The great and good, royalty and nobility displayed the full range of emotional and political attachments. We tend to remember that Victoria was devoted to Albert; the first Elizabeth was something of a tease; Charles II had a mistress called Nell Gwynne; and Edward VII was fond of actresses who called him Bertie.

The lower orders, meanwhile, were left largely to get on with life and love as best they could. Passion never went out of fashion, and men and women took what pleasures they could in a short and harsh life. Romances and passions might last as long as life itself, fade quietly away, or be destroyed in sudden anger. But love has remained a constant force – in its unpredictable and chaotic way – throughout the ages.

May you both live happily ever after.

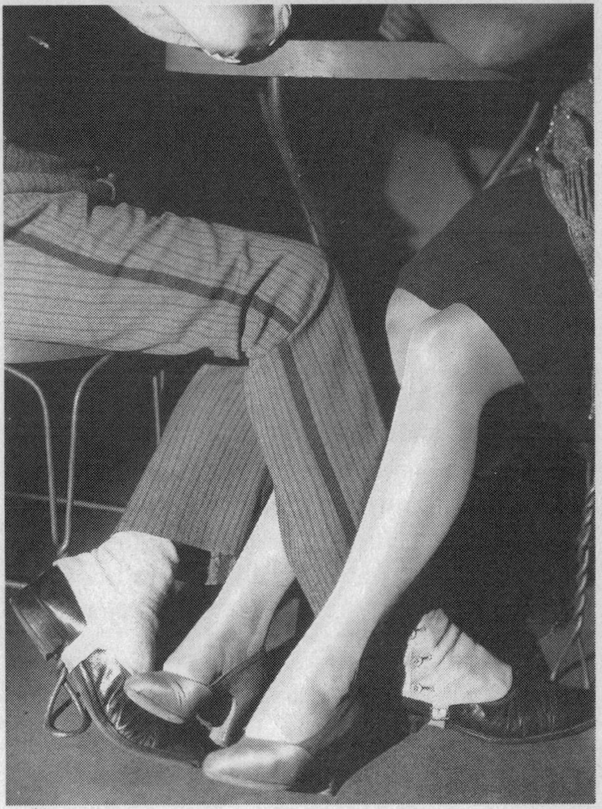

Love Story

Romance Through the Ages

Love and marriage, the late Frank Sinatra told us back in 1956, go together like a horse and carriage. It's a nice thought, but one with little basis in historical fact. You can have one without the other, and usually did, throughout history and in most countries. The concept of a marriage based on the mutual attraction of two young lovers is a comparatively recent phenomenon. Otherwise, marriage has been regarded as a practical matter, a business transaction. Marriage was a contract. Love, if it happened at all, came later. The couple themselves had no say in the matter, and would only have met each other previously by accident. Such bargains would often be sealed when the couple were still infants. Moreover, once the contract was agreed, they would usually be kept from each other until the bargain was sealed and solemnised.

'Love comes after marriage' was a common saying, quoted by Plutarch in the first century and, according to a Victorian textbook, love is 'common among the Esquimaux savages'.

Yet love, in one form or another, is the catalyst that turned primitive human beings from savages to members of an organised and structured society, based on the family unit. As an instinct it is less basic and fundamental only than the instinct to survive.

This original concept of marriage, which can still be found among the more affluent today, had its basis in the improvement of the wealth, power and influence of families. It was entirely too weighty a matter to be left to chance in the hands of emotionally unstable and inexperienced youth.

But love could not be crushed out of existence, and it emerges as the fulcrum of literature, a powerful force that has no basis in reason and causes rash acts which have profound influences on history. Love, according to Plato, was 'a divine madness'.

> 'Men always want to be a woman's first love – women like to be a man's last romance.'
> Oscar Wilde

Nevertheless it is difficult to reconcile the general view of the ancient Greeks, as with most cultures of the time – that the wife occupied a place little higher than a slave in the husband's household, and was regarded as a possession – with countless moving passages in the earliest 'novels' of Homer. These detail love in all its many aspects – pure lust for Helen of Troy; the deep affection of Achilles for his cousin and inseparable companion Patroclus; the patient faithfulness of Odysseus's wife Penelope, sitting by the tapestry she secretly unpicked each night, to fend off the band of suitors who hoped to usurp her lost husband's place.

The Dial, Arthur Hughes, 1871; Ashmolean Museum, Oxford.

In the Roman empire, women gradually came to play a more significant role in society, able to own property in their own right, and occupying positions of power and authority. Love, too, continued to flourish, with several religious ceremonies specifically connected with carnal desire. The Bacchanalia, for instance, degenerated into an excuse for an orgy, and were eventually suppressed.

The early Christian church had a difficult task, taking a moralistic stance against the fabled hedonism of the Romans. The simple virtues of chastity and abstinence might be thought to hold little attraction. It also has to be said, that in general terms and for most of history, the concept of chastity has generally been applied somewhat more rigorously to women than to men. A popular sixteenth-century French handbook advocated the use of a small sac of sheep's blood as proof of virginity for the newly-wed girl. Early Christians, meanwhile, would practise chaste but close unions between young couples, sleeping together but resisting the greatest temptation of all.

It was indirectly from this practice that the notion of courtly love arose, in southern France at the end of the eleventh century. Courtly love came to be epitomised by Dante's love for Beatrice: such a passion was by definition quite hopeless and would never be consummated in marriage. A conveniently unobtainable object of the courtly affections, however, was a married woman: Lancelot's Guinevere, for instance. Courtly love often failed to meet its own ideals, and adultery became commonplace. But for a medieval knight the chief object of life was the pursuit of love, and many of its tenets form the basis of that concept of romantic love to which we all aspire.

> 'The function of courtship is to give young people who think they are in love a real chance to find out whether they really are. A courtship of reasonable duration provides evidence upon which to make the vital decision of putting one's all into a partnership.'
>
> From *Adolescence to Maturity*,
> V. C. Chamberlain, Penguin, 1959

Before the Norman invasion, which was eventually to import this French ideal of courtly love, Anglo-Saxons seemed to be more interested in drink than love or even sex. Existing stories and poems all centre around excessive consumption of alcohol. The most common relic archaeologists retrieve from this period is the drinking horn. Subtle love-making was unlikely to flourish in such an atmosphere.

My Pigsney

A medieval term of endearment. Literally, 'my pig's eye'. Pigs were an important part of the medieval economy: pigs and their litter were symbolic of fertility. They actually appeared on early British coins.

The church had officially outlawed incest in the seventh century, and passed a decree allowing a woman to remarry if the husband had been captured.

A passionate exchange between Vilma Banky and Rudolph Valentino in *The Son of the Sheik*, 1926.

Previously, husbands could divorce for reasons of a wife's barrenness, or if she were 'deformed, fetid, silly, passionate, rude, a glutton, drunkard, quarrelsome or abusive'. Moderate corporal punishment was allowed, defined in one law as three blows with a broomstick on any part of the person except the head.

Handfasting was the earliest form of marriage, where each party took the other by the hand and publicly declared themselves married. Viking invaders had introduced a form of marriage simply conducted by the bride's father. But in all its essentials, the medieval church marriage was virtually identical in wording to today's. Brides originally had their hair shorn to symbolise servitude, but later just wore it up.

William the Conqueror arrived too early to be influenced by courtly ideals of love and romance. He is supposed to have beaten up Matilda after she refused his advances. This grotesque courtship apparently put an end to her opposition and won her over. Wife beating is still a fairly common occurrence in Chaucer's works, though to be fair, it is the wife who is just as likely to be doling out the punishment. A misericord seat in Westminster Abbey depicts a woman laying into a man with a stick.

The true beginnings of modern, romantic love are to be found from the sixteenth century on. The Renaissance ideal of the triumph of the individual, science and reason and great discoveries were changing the way people lived and thought. They were inquisitive and restless: it was an age of adventure and discovery, echoed by advances in art, music and lyrical poetry. There was a flowering of the love of language for its own sake – the art of conversation, the most elegant of chat-up lines, which reached their apogee in the sonnets of Shakespeare.

The British were influenced by events and fashions on the continent, especially by the Italian and French styles. Clothes of the time were designed to attract the opposite sex: men appeared in leggings with codpieces; women's breasts were heavily padded, pushed-up, and almost exposed. Wigs, padding, perfumes, ornament and make-up were in abundance.

> During the seventeenth century, fornication was a felony, and acts of public penance during Morning Prayer for sexual offences became more frequent. A girl who had been found 'engaged in illicit carnal relations' was required to parade clothed in white, and carrying a white sheet, bare-headed, bare-legged and barefoot, in front of the congregation.

To be a virgin was simply unfashionable. Shakespeare disapprovingly referred to them as 'withered roses'. Marriage for a girl at 12 was still common: Juliet was only 14. Occasionally the couple marrying would be so young their parents would be obliged to hold them at the altar and say the vows on their behalf.

In a brief dash through history it would be easy to say the period up to the Civil War was a slow drop into constant debauchery, and the aim of the Puritans was to put an end to all such fun. That was very much a side issue in the fight for political power. All the same, the Puritans did close the theatres, and ale-houses. They even replaced church ceremonies with a dull civil marriage, and tried to ban the use of wedding rings. They legislated by the Bible, or at least their interpretation of it. Adultery became a capital offence. Christmas Day was deemed a fast day. Dancing was denounced.

The pendulum swung back, and then some, with the Restoration. Charles II led by example with his many mistresses including Nell Gwynne, and the lesser known but entirely more familiar Frances Stewart, who posed as Britannia for the coin of the realm. Samuel Pepys – 'music and women I cannot but give way to, whatever my business is' – chronicled the age.

> **'Cupid's Hotel',**
> **or**
> **'Cupid's Arms'**
> 19th century slang expression for the female genitals.

The eighteenth century was all sweet reason: trade and commerce the order of the day. The human form, like the buildings of the day, took on a staid and perfectly proportioned elegance. The waltz provided a perfect opportunity to pass a few minutes in the intimate company of the partner of your choice.

A dangerous liaison: Faye Dunaway and Warren Beatty as passionate lovers and ruthless criminals Bonnie and Clyde in the 1967 film.

Jane Austen caught the modern mood declaring that marriage without love was an awful thing: 'How wretched and unpardonable, how hopeless and how wicked it was to marry without affection,' she wrote in *Mansfield Park*.

The Romantics threw all caution to the wind; they were dying for love, which had become a violent passion. 'Love is free!' cried Shelley. 'To promise for ever to love the same woman is no less absurd than to promise to believe the same creed.' The Prince Regent was supposed to have rolled on the floor in a burst of passion when he thought he'd lost Mrs Fitzherbert.

Love tokens were taken seriously. Lord Raglan, on having his arm amputated at Waterloo, still insisted the ring his wife had given him was found.

Most modern of them all was Victoria: she proposed to Albert. Victoria also declared that women should

> 'Take the dried genital of a turtle, monkey or otter. Crush to a powder. Mix with the root of the herb marapuana and the fruit of the plants puxuri and noz-moscada. Shake well and take a little each morning for heightened desire. Or take the private parts of a male or female dolphin, depending on your sex. Mix in a glass of alcohol or sugar. Take as required. If you are a woman, substitute camphor for sugar and take a bath afterwards. For heightened pleasure.'
>
> From *Sex Appeal* by Kate and Douglas Botting

be mothers. She certainly devoted herself to the cause – in the course of her 20-year marriage she had nine children. But love, like Victorian architecture, was all façade. Everything looked fine and proper from the front; but out of public sight, were all the pipes and plumbing. Victorian prudery concealed an obsession with sex. Statues were draped and modestly covered, even table legs covered up. Prostitution was rife, which meant men like Gladstone found a mission in saving fallen women.

In all, it was something of a relief when Edward came to the throne after the seemingly interminable Victorian era. However, it was not his accession, but the First World War which put an end to innocence, changed the world forever and opened the door to the liberation of women.

Lipstick, Powder and Paint

The Things We Do for Love

The history of love throughout civilisation can be most clearly seen through the ever-changing language of fashion and personal tastes. The clothes people wear have always been considerably more than mere protection against the elements. They speak volumes about the person you are, or perhaps would like to be. Most of all they speak eloquently of the morals and culture of the age. The ancient Greeks, it might be noted, hardly distinguished between male and female fashions. But then in matters of love, to a large extent, neither did the men.

Like lovers' whims, fashions have always been flighty, ephemeral. One age admires a 'prettily turned ankle', another, large and voluptuous ladies. Women have accentuated and even exposed their breasts, or flattened them to boyish dimensions. Bottoms too have been subject to grotesque distortions in the Victorian

Charming

How to win your love (and get arrested...):
The lover should burn, at a cross-roads, at the moon's first quarter, a model moulded from the hair, saliva, blood and nail parings of the beloved. She then urinates on that spot, repeating, 'X, I love you. When your image shall have perished, you will follow me as a dog a bitch.' Thereafter her victim will enjoy no peace, except at her side.

bustle. Sixteenth-century men flaunted themselves in tights and codpieces: like so many fashions, more illusion than reality, promising more than they could ever deliver.

Medieval women shaved their foreheads to give themselves an intellectual air. In sixteenth-century France it was for a brief period the fashion to shave all body hair. A few years later, however, it became popular to encourage its growth: people would even put pomade on their nether regions to encourage hair growth and enable decorative curling.

The Middle Ages found a particular attraction in a prominent rounded female belly, apparently, if not actually pregnant, like the wife in Van Eyck's *The Arnolfini Marriage*. Rubens and Titian liked them bigger still. Other ages have constricted their womenfolk in whalebone corsets.

Faces were painted deathly white with injurious and occasionally fatal lead-based compounds, or heavily rouged. Face paint was caked on to disguise the ravages of smallpox: smaller scars could be emphasised as 'beauty spots'. Men, even more than women, took to wearing absurd and often enormous wigs.

This century has seen a rapid acceleration of changing tastes. The voluptuous ideal of the fifties – Marilyn Monroe, Diana Dors – gave way to the waif-like Twiggy of the sixties. Hemlines moved up and down with barometric regularity. Beards and moustaches in different decades tell very different stories.

Even the humble tie is supposed to carry a certain hint of male prowess. That is palpably true in the case of the macho seventies, which favoured grotesque 'kipper' ties. Less clear is the interpretation of a demure spotted bow tie or, more to the point, the leather bootlaces affected by besuited cowboys. It has to be noted, however, that the clergy have long disdained the wearing of ties altogether.

> **'Men love with their eyes, women love with their ears.'**
> Oscar Wilde

The strange and exotic has long held a fascination for would-be lovers. The Crusades held the additional attraction of access to exotic consorts and initiation into the eastern arts of love.

The Chinese, like the Arabs and Spanish found women's feet their most erotic feature. The Inquisition forbade their 'lewd' representation in art on pain of excommunication. The Virgin Mary, for instance, would never show her feet in nativity scenes. The Chinese prized tiny feet in women so highly, that for centuries, until the Communist Revolution, the feet of baby girls were bound, and prevented from growing normally, an increasingly agonising procedure which destroyed the bone structure, and made walking all but impossible.

They didn't join Dateline

Maybe that's why they're extinct

New theory suggests that the reason dinosaurs became extinct 65 million years ago is due to misunderstanding of, and their suspicion surrounding computer dating. But the evolution of humans and the advancement of technology has proved this method to be the most successful way to meet people.

DATELINE BRINGS PEOPLE TOGETHER

People who meet through Dateline tend to form long lasting relationships — and you don't have to be prehistoric to join. Whatever your age, social background or geographical location, Dateline is a fun, affordable and exciting way to meet people.

Whether you are looking for new friends or a partner for life, Dateline could be for you

Please send me more information about Dateline.
I would also like information on Dateline Gold ☐
another way for me to meet people.
NAME..................................
ADDRESS..............................
....
....
POSTCODE .... AGE.........

POST this coupon in confidence and without any obligation TODAY

Dateline
23 Abingdon Road,
London W8 6AL
Tel: 071 938 1011

A different method of finding love; a 1993 Dateline advert.

All this in the name of tradition and fashion, and attracting the opposite sex. Emphasising, or often hiding, the parts of the body that were considered erotic. It was purely a surface thing.

Love – true love – is what made affection and devotion possible through the stench that affected most people in an age where personal hygiene was basic or non-existent. It was real love that meant that two people with mouths full of stumps and rotting teeth might still kiss, or run their hands through the lank, greasy, flea- and lice-infested hair that lay beneath the elegant powdered wigs.

> **The Elizabethans believed that every orgasm cost them a day off their lives.**

Legendary Lovers

Pyramus and Thisbe

This doomed couple were young neighbours in ancient Babylon. Forbidden by their parents to meet, they nevertheless contrived to fall in love, and pursued their romance through a tiny crack in the party wall. They resolved eventually to run away, and meet each other beyond the city under a mulberry tree by a pool they knew. Thisbe left first, heavily veiled. She reached the spot but found a lion drinking after a recent kill. She ran and hid, losing her veil, which the lion tore to shreds with its bloody claws. Pyramus now arrived, only to find the gruesome remains of his lover's veil. Cursing himself for coming too late, he stabbed himself with his sword. Blood spurted out and stained the mulberry fruits, which till then had been pure white. Thisbe now returned to find him dying, and she, too, fell on his sword, praying with her dying breath that the mulberry fruit might forever keep its dark red colour in memory of these two unlucky lovers.

Echo and Narcissus

The ultimate tale of hopeless, unrequited love. Echo was an excessively voluble young nymph, whose speech, as punishment, was restricted to repeating the last words she heard. She fell in love with the most beautiful man on earth, the haughty Narcissus, who would have nothing to do with her: he ignored her as he had countless others who loved him. Echo pined away: only her voice remained in wild and solitary places as a warning to other impulsive maidens. One of his many spurned lovers prayed that Narcissus too might know the pangs of unrequited love. When he stopped at a pool he became hopelessly infatuated with an underwater spirit that he could never quite touch. It seemed to love him – when he stretched out his hand, the spirit did the same, but it disappeared as soon as he disturbed the water. Unable to consummate this reflected love, Narcissus too pined away eventually stabbing himself. From his spilt blood grew the first narcissus, used by the Greeks, apparently, as a cure for earache and frostbite.

Orpheus and Eurydice

Orpheus was the greatest poet and musician in ancient Greece. His lyre could enchant wild beasts and cause stones and trees to follow him. He fell in love with and married Eurydice. One day she was bitten by a snake. Its bite was fatal. Orpheus decided to use his talent to win her back. Playing his lyre enabled him to get past Cerberus, the dog guarding the gates of the Underworld, and to be ferried with Charon across the Styx. His playing even melted the heart of King Tartarus, Hades himself. He agreed to release her on the sole condition that Eurydice follow Orpheus without him once looking back. She followed the sound of his playing through the pitch-dark pathways of the Underworld, and from time to time he would stop and listen for her footsteps. Finally, at the very edge of the world, he stopped, but could hear nothing. In panic he turned, caught sight of her, and she was lost to him forever. Orpheus lost all interest in music, life and women. His disinterest offended the Maenads, disciples of Dionysus, who attacked him and tore him to pieces. They flung his head into the river Hebrus, which floated, still singing, down to the sea and as far as the island of Lesbos.

Cupid and Psyche

This ancient story, first told by Apuleius, contains the main elements of the popular fairy stories 'Beauty and the Beast', 'Cinderella', 'Sleeping Beauty' and even 'Rumpelstiltskin'. A king had three daughters. Psyche was the youngest and by far the most beautiful. People were so obsessed with her beauty they thought she must be Venus herself. This offended the goddess and she sent her mischievous son Cupid to make her fall in love with some vile beast. But Cupid himself was smitten, and took her to a secret palace, where he would only come to her at night, invisible. Her jealous sisters convinced Psyche that her secret lover was really a gruesome reptile, and that she should kill him. But by the light of her lamp she saw that her lover was the winged Cupid who, enraged, left her: she was pregnant with his unborn child. In shame, she tried to kill herself by jumping from a cliff, but a river saved her. The jealous sisters believed Cupid had caught Psyche and whisked her away. So they too jumped from the cliffs – but were dashed to pieces on the rocks below. Venus punished Psyche

'Eros', one of London's most photographed statues.

with a series of impossible tasks, such as sorting out mountains of grain in a single night, but the ants took pity on her and helped her. She fetched golden wool; black water from the river Styx; and a box of beauty from the Queen of the Underworld, Proserpine, with divine help. Eventually Venus relented, and the couple were reunited in Olympus, where Psyche gave birth to a daughter, Pleasure.

Eros

The figure who looks down on the crowds in Piccadilly Circus was designed and cast in aluminium in 1893 by Sir Alfred Gilbert. The statue, on top of a fountain, was erected in memory of the philanthropist Lord Shaftesbury. Today, surrounded by advertising hoardings, jostling crowds, permanent traffic jams and diesel fumes, it's hardly the most romantic of locations. But the statue actually represents not Eros at all, but 'The Angel of Christian Charity': Eros was merely a popular misconception.

Casanova

Giovanni Giacomo Casanova di Seingalt, was a Venetian adventurer and occasional author in the eighteenth century. He travelled around Europe earning his living from gambling, spying, writing and seducing women. He was convicted of 'impiety and magical practices' and locked up in the Venice State prison. Escaping from there, he made his way to France, became director of the Paris lottery and amassed a fortune. He retired to the castle of Dux in

Bohemia as librarian. His amorous reputation is founded largely on his memoirs, which were only published in full in 1960.

Don Juan

It would be a most insensitive fellow these days who would describe himself as 'a bit of a Don Juan'. The original character, Don Juan Tenorio, was created by Tirso de Molin in the seventeenth century. Many versions exist of his story, and he may or may not be based on one of a number of actual people. Don Juan seduced the daughter of the commander of Seville and killed her father in a duel. Rather rudely, he invited the statue of his victim to join him at a feast. The outraged and insulted statue came to life and dragged him off to Hell.

Tristan and Isolde

The story of Tristan and Isolde was embroidered and retold throughout the Middle Ages as the very essence of courtly love: an adulterous, impossible affair conducted in a state of idealism and purity. Tristan was a prince of Lyonesse, a legendary land off the coast of Cornwall. He was sent on an errand by King Mark of Cornwall to escort Isolde back from Ireland to marry the king. Isolde's maid had prepared a love potion for the royal couple to drink after their marriage, but Tristan and Isolde drank this by accident during the voyage. Naturally, they fell hopelessly in love, despite Isolde's discovery that Tristan had killed her father – she had kept a piece of his sword that had lodged in his skull and Tristan's sword had a piece missing that matched the shard. Tristan had also been wounded in Ireland after slaying a dragon there. Isolde possessed the power of healing and had saved his life.

Isolde married King Mark, despite her feelings. It is said she sent a maid to the royal bed in her place. She contrived to meet with Tristan, and their chaste passion flourished. Finding them asleep together, Tristan's sword between the lovers, King Mark replaced it with his own. Tristan awoke, realised they had been discovered, and left for voluntary exile in France. Despairing of consummating his passion for Isolde, he married – another Isolde. Mortally wounded in battle, he sent a ship to bring the original Isolde over to cure him. A signal was arranged that the ship would hoist white sails if she came, black if she refused. Too ill to look, Tristan asked his wife the colour of the sail. She lied, saying it was black. Tristan died. Finding him dead, the original Isolde died with him. The lovers, separated in life, were united in death. From their grave two trees grew, inextricably entwined.

Love: It's Magic

Romantic Spells and Superstitions

> **CAUTION:**
> Love potions, spells and other varieties of 'magic' are undertaken solely at your own risk!

Love is the most ancient, most bewitching, most fantastic of emotions. Its effects on the individual are magical; and it is thus not surprising that love should be surrounded by superstition and legend. The traditions which surround love are almost as old as the emotion itself, and date back to ancient times when people believed passionately in spells and incantation. Folklore, legend and myth: love rolls them all together to produce some riveting and revolting pieces of sorcery and tradition. Not all love traditions exist only in the past, either: many of them are still thriving today, although in a very different form.

Potent Potions

The origins of love potions date back many hundreds of years, to the ancient lore of plants and other natural remedies. Women who knew the properties of various plants were often labelled 'witches'; but when witchcraft – and the fear of it – faded at the end of the seventeenth century the secrets were passed on to, and left with, the gypsies.

Many love potions or spells are based on scientific fact – in a roundabout way. Most of them involve implanting your blood, sweat, saliva (or worse) into the person you love – either literally or metaphorically. This symbolically binds the two lovers, forming a solid and unshakeable physical link. The other aspect of these potions is pheromones – those hormonal secretions which mysteriously attract members of the opposite sex and which are found in sweat and other bodily excretions. Such chemicals are probably also at the bottom of aphrodisiacs and other legendary concoctions designed to induce love.

> ### Blood Lust
>
> In rural Oklahoma, a man could win a woman's love by putting a drop of blood onto a sweet for her; she could win his by dropping some of her menstrual blood into his whisky.

Other love spells are founded on the mystical properties of certain plants. In the Swiss Alps, nigritella or 'man's troth' was placed under the pillow, or into the pocket, to make a man or woman fall in love. In parts of the US and Africa, wild verbena, or vervain (which has very magical powers) used to be planted at the door to attract lovers.

Revenge Is Sweet

Of course, it'll never happen: you'll be together forever. But just in case – here are some good old-fashioned vengeance spells:

Valentine Guardian

LUMP UP THOSE pillows, just come live with me and my love.

SQUIRREL – LOOKING forward to the next lunchtime. I'll bring the nuts. Lots of fond. M.

To the girl who got on the 52 bus
in Neasden High Street
at quarter past eight last Friday,
and sat upstairs three seats
from the back.
You were pretty as a picture
(but I hadn't
got my camera with me).

You can never be sure what you'll see.
But you can always be sure of a Sure Shot.

— Canon —

- In the southern US, they used to destroy relationships by taking the tracks of a man and his wife (that's the earth on which they trod) and putting them in a paper bag. This was then burnt, together with the whiskers of a cat and dog.

- In Yugoslavia, if you seek vengeance, you should mix crabshell with the food of the faithless lover. The individual will pine for you thereafter, and will endure a wretched relationship with their current partner.

The Future's Bright

For hundreds of years, people have been trying to find out ways of 'seeing' their future partner. This is one tradition which isn't confined solely to the past: open up any teenage magazine, and the horoscopes will be pointing you towards the ideal partner, whilst 'compatibility charts' have always been popular. Still, there's no doubt about it, the old ways of finding out who you'd end up with were much more unusual.

- In Arkansas, they had the 'dumb supper'. Two girls had to stay silent for an evening, and not consume any food. They then had to bake a loaf of bread made from cornmeal, salt and spring water, and leave it out in the kitchen. Future husbands would, apparently, enter the room to 'turn' the cake, and all doors and windows had to be left open for them.

- In medieval times, the Eve of St Agnes (20 January) was a very important date in any English girl's calendar. On the evening before St Agnes's Day, a virgin would be given a vision of her future love whilst sleeping.

Flowery Gifts

In England in times past, flowers were the most popular present to give your beloved. Gifts were fairly thin on the ground during winter and autumn: but girls were absolutely swamped at harvest time. The Irish were big on 'harvest knots'; the Scots made brooches. The Dutch were rather uninspired, giving cake moulds or spoons; other Europeans used to give women needle sheaths (apparently, these had great erotic significance!).

Of all the flowers, honeysuckle was the least popular: parents used to forbid it being brought indoors, in case it gave their daughters erotic dreams.

In the nineteenth century particularly, when lovers could not express their emotions without fear of being thought immoral, flowers served a real purpose. Every bouquet had a special meaning, and a blushing

> ### The Witching Hour
>
> On Hallowe'en, you should name a handful of nuts for different lovers (making sure the shells are still on) and lay them on the hearth, whilst reciting the rhyme:
>
> *If you love me, pop and fly*
> *If not, lie there silently.*

lover could use it to tell the woman of his dreams how he really felt.

The Language of Flowers

Amaryllis	*Splendid beauty*
Burdock	*Touch me not*
Buttercup	*Childishness*
Carnation	*Love*
Crocus	*Do not abuse me*
Daffodil	*Regard*
Daisy	*Innocence*
Dandelion	*Love's oracle*
Heather	*Luck*
Ivy	*Eternal fidelity*
Lotus Flower	*Estranged love*
Marigold	*Grief*
Orange blossom	*Fertility and happiness*
Parsley	*Knowledge*
Pansy	*Thoughts*
Red rose	*I love you*
Violet	*Faithfulness*

The flowers may be combined and arranged in different ways to form a very precise statement. Responses to a question posed by a bouquet can be formed thus: touching the flower to the lips implies 'yes'; removing a petal and throwing it away implies 'no'.

Auguste Rodin, *The Kiss*, 1901–4; Tate Gallery, London.

Pucker Up

The History Of Kissing

The Romans had three words for kiss, differentiating between kisses of greeting, affection, and love. The Japanese, so it is said, had no word for it at all.

Anthropologists encountered nose-rubbing rituals in the frozen north and the tropics. Darwin referred to it as the 'Malayan' kiss. Kissing would seem to be unknown in ancient Egypt, but was ubiquitous in ancient Greece. Whether or not kissing developed a symbolic usage, in primitive societies, kissing between mothers and their babies was the most natural expression of maternal love and close contact.

While such physical contact gradually became an almost universal expression of physical affection, the kiss developed symbolic meanings in parallel. In Greece, inferiors kissed the knees, hand or breast of a superior. In Persia, equals kissed on the mouth, near

Sealed With A Kiss

What to put on the backs of those love letters:

SWALK	Sealed with a loving kiss
SWANK	Sealed with a nice kiss
BOLTUP	Better on lips than upon paper
HOLLAND	Hope our love lasts and never dies
ITALY	I trust and love you
BURMA	Be undressed ready my angel
NORWICH	(K)nickers off ready when I come home

social equals on the cheek, while one inferior in rank threw himself on the floor. Kissing the feet is a demonstration of humiliation before a superior.

For Hebrews in biblical times, inferiors would again kiss the hand of a superior. Judas would not have kissed Jesus on the face: it would have been socially impossible.

Persons elected to office, knights dubbed, all used the kiss to seal and formalise the ceremony. Medieval knights kissed before combat, much as latter-day boxers still touch gloves. Reconciled enemies kissed symbolically to signify that hostilities were at an end.

The Renaissance practice of kissing the hand as a mark of respect has remained amongst royalty, as has the even more specialised kissing of the Pope's ring.

Social kissing in England declined after the Renaissance; the act was restricted to parents and lovers. Kissing between friends of opposite sex fell out of fashion, as it already had on the continent. Congreve, at the end of seventeenth century wrote: 'In the country, where great lubberly brothers slabber and kiss one another when they meet: 'tis not the fashion here'.

Nevertheless, it became fashionable once more on the continent long before the recent and bizarre ritual of 'air kissing' in this country and the USA. But while friends might kiss on the continent without any raised eyebrows, for the more restrained British, two men

> **'The moist lips are batteries charged with our very inmost good or evil.'**
> Eulis, *Affectional Alchemy*, 1930

kissing is restricted to the football field and the company of consenting adults.

The childish rite of 'blowing a kiss' also has very ancient origins. It was once the customs of Turks to kiss their own hand and place that kiss on another. The breath, according to folklore, was the essence of life, even the soul. Ancient people sent out their kisses, their life, to the things they worshipped – the sun and moon. A kiss, in folklore, imparted magic powers – in fairy tales a kiss changed an enchanted frog, or dragon, into a prince. Waking the Sleeping Beauty might just have some realistic basis in the 'kiss of life'.

Kissing, for Christians, has long formed part of solemn rites. A kiss might be enough to indicate betrothal – a solemn pact, the initiation of marriage, and not undertaken lightly. Kissing a deceased

> **'To love is to suffer. To avoid suffering one must not love. But then one suffers from not loving. Therefore, to love is to suffer; not to love is to suffer; to suffer is to suffer. To be happy is to love. To be happy, then, is to suffer, but suffering makes one unhappy. Therefore, to be happy one must love or love to suffer or suffer from too much happiness.'**
> Woody Allen

'Here's looking at you, kid.' Humphrey Bogart and Ingrid Bergman in *Casablanca*, 1942.

relative was a formal farewell. Penitents were kissed as a mark of forgiveness, as was the Prodigal Son on his return. Early Christians placed immense importance on the kiss of peace as an expression of their beliefs. This was exploited by Romans who would force them to kiss pagan effigies. Ancient Greeks wore away statues with religious kisses – as Catholics and Muslims still do today. Kissing an ancient relic or saintly effigy was believed to cure illness. We still talk of 'kissing it better' about a child's grazed knee. Many religions incorporate kissing of ceremonial robes as they are put on. Kissing the Bible was an ancient way of taking an oath, sealed by physical contact. Today one may not take an oath in court holding the Bible in a gloved hand.

Religion and kissing remain inextricably linked. It may well not be accidental that we still denote kisses on letters with crosses.

Mistletoe

Mistletoe, according to legend, was once a free-standing tree, and it was from mistletoe wood that the Cross was built. From then on it was condemned to its parasitic existence. But its religious associations are far older: it is most closely associated with the Druids, and is the 'Golden Bough' that Sir James Frazer wrote of in his seminal work on mythology, magic and religion. It features strongly in Norse mythology, and the story of the god Balder who could only be killed – and was – by an arrow of mistletoe wood. It may well be this legend that was incorporated into Christian tradition.

The Druids maintained a strict ritual for its collection and use to fend off evil. Mistletoe growing in oak was the most powerful, and must only be cut with a golden knife, and not allowed to fall to the ground.

These associations, and the mystery of its existence high among the branches of fruit and oak trees, have long imbued it with supposed magical powers. Culpeper, the herbalist, claimed that when worn around the neck it protected the wearer against witchcraft. Celts believed it could cure several conditions, including, according to Pliny, tumours and epilepsy. It was also thought to prevent poisoning, although mistletoe berries contain toxic compounds that are in themselves poisonous to humans.

> 'A kiss without a moustache is like an egg without salt.'
> (Old Spanish saying)

Its most powerful and persistent use has been as a fertility symbol, both for livestock and for people. Because of its strong pagan associations, its use as a church decoration was long banned. It is used to this day to bring luck to the household and lovers, and is hung in houses throughout Europe and the United States at Christmas.

It signifies permission to kiss, traditionally as many kisses as there are berries on the sprig. Once, indeed, a gentleman would remove one berry for each kiss obtained. The sprig, with or without its berries must be removed from the house after Twelfth Night and burned, or all the couples who kissed under that sprig will be enemies by the end of the year.

You can be a great lover

It comes natural to men, even great hulking plain men, to be lovers of BRITVIC Pure Fruit Juices. Any other sort of great love may easily pall, but BRITVIC Orange, Tomato, Grapefruit and Pineapple juices in those modestly priced little bottles inspire constant affection. You can make such delicious cocktails with BRITVIC fruit juices and, if you're too lazy to do your own shaking, there is a ready-mixed BRITVIC Tomato cocktail that you can decant and pass off as your own.

Send for your FREE copy of 'How to tell a good cocktail'

Our cocktail recipe booklet is feebly humorous and most awfully instructive with lashings of illustrations. You will be able to mix soul-stirring cocktails in a jiffy—or if you have no jiffy, in a shaker.

BritviC

Write now to :—
The British Vitamin Products Ltd. (Dept. 169), West House, Broomfield Road, Chelmsford, Essex.

Helpful advice from a 1952 Britvic advertisement.

The Food Of Love

Aphrodisiacs Through The Ages

The Greeks had a word for it: for them, music alone wasn't the food of love. The word aphrodisiac is directly associated, naturally enough, with the name of their god of love, beauty and fertility, Aphrodite, who was known to the Romans as Venus. She originally emerged from the sea foam, standing naked in a scallop shell, her birth the accidental result of the god Uranus being attacked by his sons, the Titans, while he slept. They castrated him, and tossed his still-fertile genitals into the sea.

> If a man cuts into small pieces the sprouts of the vajna-sunhi plant, and dips them into a mixture of red arsenic and sulphur and then dries them seven times, mixes them with honey and burns them at night, and if, looking at the smoke, he sees a golden moon behind, he will be successful with any woman, and if he throws some of the powder mixed with the excrement of a monkey upon a maiden, she will not be given in marriage to anybody else.
>
> From *Sex Appeal* by Kate and Douglas Botting

It was Aphrodite who won the first beauty contest, beating Hera and Athene to win the golden apple, by bribing the judge Paris with the promise of the beautiful Helen. And Helen abandoned her husband Menelaus, thus starting the Trojan War.

An aphrodisiac, of course, is a food, or potion or anything that stimulates, or at least is believed to stimulate, sexual passion. In odd cases there are valid and scientifically demonstrable reasons for this. But for the most part the effect is purely that of a placebo. It is the belief that it will work that has the desired effect, or a crude association of shape or function.

And just as effective are the implications behind the possession of such aids. The best aphrodisiacs of all are rare, exotic and horrendously expensive.

> **'A well-fed stomach and a naked body breed lust in a man.'**
> Chinese proverb

Their possession implies, or rather demonstrates, substantial wealth, and the inclination to spend it rashly. Throughout history such attributes have been inherently, and deeply, sexy.

So the unfortunate rhinoceros has been hunted almost to extinction because of the accident of evolution that left him with an erect protuberance on his snout.

The sight of blood was a more common stimulant. If you wanted to find a brothel in ancient Rome, the first place to look was next to the circus where gladiators fought, and lions devoured early Christians.

The most famous aphrodisiac of all, Spanish fly, is obtained from the crushed remains of the cantharides beetle. Applied to the genitals it is, we are told, an irritant, and causes swelling. All well and good, but it pays to read the instructions carefully. Taken internally it is usually fatal.

Just as ancient tribes ate the remains of their enemies to acquire their power and enhance their own, so the Romans would partake of the genitals of various animals to boost their post-prandial performance. Oysters and figs may well owe their popularity to a perceived resemblance to female genitalia.

And the list is endless. The humble potato was once a rare and expensive import. The tomato was once known as the 'love apple'. Truffles, ginger, rocket lettuce, sandalwood, cummin seed, candies, citrus fruits, marigolds, cloves, egg-yolks, bananas, the testicles of cocks, and shrimps all figure in various accounts. The only surprise is that cucumber, despite its suggestive appearance, is universally agreed to have the opposite effect.

Cinematic Slush

1. *Love Story*
2. *Romeo and Juliet*
3. *West Side Story*
4. *Brief Encounter*
5. *Casablanca*
6. *Breakfast at Tiffany's*
7. *Endless Love*
8. *An Officer and a Gentleman*
9. *Sleepless in Seattle*
10. *When Harry Met Sally*

Hormonally Yours

Sexy Science

Love: it's a complex thing. For centuries scientists, philosophers and other 'experts' have been trying to ascertain what makes us fall in love, and why it should have such a powerful affect upon us. Unsurprisingly, the only conclusion that anyone has been able to draw is that love is a product of thousands of years of evolution, combined with the basic need to reproduce.

Romantic love would seem to be an abstract concept; but there's no doubt about it, some of the effects are definitely physical. Trembling knees, pounding heart, churning stomach: all these are very real, very passionate, but rather uncomfortable symptoms experienced by Cupid's latest casualties. They're caused by the hormones and chemicals which are flooding your nervous system and creating all those jittery and excited feelings.

The physical side of love and sexual attraction is a complicated process, and a speedy one. When the lover sees the loved one, thousands of messages are sent to the brain, which leaps into action:

> **'Sexual indulgence before the age of 25 not only retards the development of the genital organs, but of the whole body, impairs the strength, injures the constitution and shortens life.'**
>
> 19th-century medical textbook

Lover Sees Loved One

SENSES GO INTO OVERDRIVE
Smell, touch, hearing, sight, taste are all sending messages to the brain at lightning speed. The pupils dilate to take in more light, hearing becomes sharper and sight more acute; other activity interprets age, status, personality, etc. Behind all this is memory and other 'association data' hard at work to categorise and compare the object of desire.

And *inside* the body

HYPOTHALAMUS
A cherry-sized organ behind the eyes which co-ordinates the hormonal system.

stimulates the...

PITUITARY GLAND
Part of the endocrine system; partly responsible for releasing the sex hormones.

released by the adrenal gland at the same time are...

of which the most important is...

ADRENALINE NORADRENALINE
Create the sensations of fear, anxiety – and also euphoria. Noradrenaline is often called the 'turn-on hormone' and is another mysterious element behind the sex drive.

TESTOSTERONE
Not just a 'male' hormone: it is found within both men and women – although in larger quantities in men – and is resonsible for much of the libido's activities.

*It is adrenaline which is responsible for those **trembling knees, sweaty palms, butterflies in the stomach, and light-headed** feelings.*

RESULT:
that this process, over in just a couple of minutes, is dominant amongst the many other factors in producing the amazing, euphoric, knee-trembling, voice-wobbling, lust-fuelled, stomach-churning physical side effects of LOVE.

It Smells To Heaven

The organ most associated with love is – in purer minds, anyway – the heart. The organ most stimulated by love, however, is probably the nose.

Although it may not register on a conscious level, smell is one of the first things we all notice about a potential lover. Smell can trigger the oldest and most intimate of memories, instantly taking us back to childhood: it has powerful emotional connotations.

> ### *Talking Dirty*
>
> **Japan's rich vocabulary of genital euphemisms includes:**
> 'Octopus'
> 'Snapping turtle'
> 'Middle leg'
> 'Scallop'
> 'Teapot'
> 'Honourable little tinkle-tinkle'

The average human has around three million scent glands in total – more than any other primate – although we no longer use them all. Most of these glands are found in the armpits, the genital area, the mouth, nose, scalp, nipples, belly button, ears and eyelids. The smell produced by the armpits contains certain steroids with musky odours, similar to the mating pheromones found in pigs.

As far as smell goes, 'pheromone' seems to be the magic word. Many people now believe that pheromones can somehow attract the individual of our dreams, if we merely waft them in his or her direction. Unfortunately, matters seem to be a little more complicated than this.

Until pheromones were identified in the late fifties, it was generally thought that animals could communicate with one another through invisible messages, but it was not known how. Now we know that a tiny amount of hormone is secreted by certain animals, which is then detected by a special receptor, thought to be in the nose, called the VNO (the vomeronasal organ). This is distinct from the general smell receptor, because it actually receives messages, thought to be connected to sexual behaviour. We know now that humans emit pheromones: but do they have a VNO? Only time will tell.

> ### The Sounds of Love
>
> According to the Kama Sutra, the most common sounds of love are cooing; weeping; 'phut'; 'phat'; 'sut'; 'plat'.

It was, of course, only a matter of time before someone started to cash in on the pheromone phenomenon. Large amounts of money have already been spent on manufacturing perfumes based on pheromones, with the aim of causing desired partners to throng around the individual in question. None, however, have proved to be particularly successful so far.

While essence of armpit might sound a revolting concoction, it should be noted that a principal constituent of most perfumes is musk. Musk is a bitter substance extracted from a gland near the genitals of the musk deer. For 11 months of the year, the musk deer browses quietly on aromatic shrubs; during the twelfth, it gives off a stink that a potential partner can detect from half a mile away. Civet is another important ingredient, taken from the anal glands of the unfortunate Ethiopian wild civet cat; together with musk, it is thought to be very similar to two of the human sex pheromones. The more conventional perfumes are one of the most romantic gifts any lover can give their loved one. It is believed that perfume can heighten and change mood, and its ability to do this is probably due to the musk which comprises the base scent of most perfumes.

Love From...?

St Valentine's Day

Poor old St Valentine was not, so far as we know, a particularly romantic chap. The history of the third century AD is complicated by the fact that there were anything up to a dozen Christian martyrs called Valentine. Further complications arise from the subsequent habit of Popes unearthing the remains of saints and giving them to various churches and religious communities. Thus various parts of several Valentines are supposedly located in Ireland, Belgium, Spain and France, as well as Rome, where the most likely candidate for *the* Saint Valentine was martyred in 269 AD.

This one was a priest and physician, arrested for having assisted the martyrs during Emperor Claudius the Goth's routine persecution of Christians. Valentine took the opportunity afforded by his confinement to preach the faith to his guard as well as restoring the sight of his daughter. The guard was converted on the spot, and was baptised with his whole family. Claudius condemned Valentine to be beheaded. This happened, of course, on 14 February.

> 'Nothing takes the taste out of peanut butter quite like unrequited love.'
> Charlie Brown

It is understandable that the physician St Valentine would come to be invoked against epilepsy, fainting and plague. By more obscure means he became the patron saint of beekeepers and travellers. But it was by complete accident of history and calendar that he also became associated with young people – and engaged couples.

The Romans had long celebrated 15 February with a slightly bizarre ritual in honour of Faunus, a Roman version of the Greek god Pan. Worshippers made their way to the Lupercal, the cave where Romulus and Remus, the founders of Rome, had been suckled by a wolf. A dog and some goats were then sacrificed, and the initiates smeared with their blood. Then, dressed in the skins of the goats – or quite naked – they would run around a prepared course, where women would stand, waiting to be scourged with thongs of goat skin and hair. This festival, known as Lupercalia, was carried out each year to ensure fertility for fields, flocks and particularly the women encountered and ritually abused on the way.

> In the 18th century, it was agreed by many that illnesses suffered by unmarried girls could be cured by copulation.

These pagan rites endured long into Christian times, and were only finally suppressed in 494. Some slight vestiges, however, endure to this day.

The strips carried by the priests were known in Latin as februa, after which the month February is named, 'the month of purification'.

St Valentine, who accidentally shared the same approximate date with the ceremony, was relegated to minor status because of this pagan taint and the lack of reliable evidence. There are no British churches, for instance, named after him. But the association remained and was reinforced by a medieval belief that all birds chose their mates on this day. And he remains one of very few saints for whom almost anyone can instantly recall the day with which he is associated.

> 'At the touch of love everyone becomes a poet.'
> Plato

The custom of sending Valentines started in the Middle Ages, and traditionally the note or message should be anonymous. The Victorians, as was their habit, imposed large doses of cloying sentiment on the practice, which was in gradual decline until revived – again for commercial reasons – after the First World War.

Today husbands and wives can buy each other specific cards and a new tradition has grown up for the broadsheets to carry pages and pages of cryptic messages featuring furry animals and baby talk, where some vestiges of anonymity are still to be found.

And each year some seven million long-stemmed red roses flood in from hothouses around the world to feed our whims, salve our consciences, and impose on florists a single day of extremely lucrative mayhem.

Whom do we have to thank for this association? High among the suspects is Robert Burns, who, without the benefit of international temperature-controlled delivery said, more practically:

> *O, my luve's like a red, red rose,*
> *That's newly sprung in June...*

Copyright Notices

Text

p.3, 14 Extracts from *Sex Appeal* by Kate and
Douglas Botting; © Boxtree, 1994.
Reproduced by kind permission of Macmillan.

Illustrations

p.3   Photograaph courtesy of Kobal the Collection.
p.6   © Ashmolean Museum, Oxford.
p.13 *Bonnie and Clyde,* © Warner Bros., 1967.
      Photograph courtesy of the Kobal Collection.
p.9   *The Son of the Sheik,* © United Artists, 1926.
      Photograph courtesy of the Kobal Collection.
p.19 © Dateline, 1993.
p.30 © *The Guardian,* 1995.
p.34 © Tate Gallery, London.
p.38 *Casablanca,* © Warner Bros., 1942.
      Photograph courtesy of the Kobal Collection.
p.42 © Britvic, 1952.

Purple House Limited has done its best to acknowledge the authors of all quotations and illustrations used in this book, but has not been able to make contact with everyone whose work is featured. If your work has not been acknowledged, please contact Purple House Limited, who will be happy to make proper acknowledgement if this book is reprinted or reissued.